relapse/slips

abstinent alcoholics
who return to drinking

relapse/slips

MAXWELL N. WEISMAN, M.D.
AND LUCY BARRY ROBE

JOHNSON INSTITUTE

ISBN: 0-935908-14-5

Printed in the United States of America

table of contents

Preface from the Johnson Institute

RELAPSE

Introduction 11
Definitions of Alcoholism 12
Denial: Cunning, Baffling, Powerful 15
Denial: Theory and Operation 17
Psychotherapy and Treatment 19
Elements of a Successful Recovery Program 21
Psychological Problems Can Affect Relapse 24
The Dry Drunk 26
Self-Knowledge and a Support System 28
A Final Word to Health Care Professionals 29
Notes 31

SLIPS, SOBRIETY, AND THE A.A. PROGRAM

Introduction 35
Attitudes Are Part of the Denial System 36
Attitudes About A.A. 41
Relapse and an Attitude of Dissatisfaction 43
Compromises Concerning A.A. 45
Twelfth Step Work 47
Other Common Pitfalls 48
The Dry Drunk 49
How Many A.A. Members Slip? 50
Bottom Lines 51

preface

For the men and women who have embarked upon a life style of sobriety — albeit one day at a time — the rewards of deliverance from alcoholism are many and large. As the months of sobriety turn into years, most men and women who are alcoholics become increasingly aware of the value of what they have discovered, and they become more and more appreciative of their new-found way of life.

The possibility of going back to drinking, however, always remains. True, as years of sobriety increase in number, the likelihood of relapse diminishes, but it never disappears completely.

The two essays that follow, one written by a psychiatrist with more than twenty-five years of experience in the field of alcoholism, and the other by a writer who has investigated alcoholism and recovery for several years, offer an interplay of ideas on how relapse begins, what signs bear watching, and what can be done to avoid it.

Professionals and the interested public alike will find these two authors' work invaluable and interesting: each essay supports and comments indirectly on the other. But in addition to all the information given and ideas suggested for consideration, there is an important concept from Bill Wilson (a co-founder of Alcoholics Anonymous) implicit in their writings. Serving the professional and nonprofessional alike, it needs to be emphasized: "Let's be friendly with our friends." This phrase was the title of a *Grapevine* article, March, 1958. Foremost, Wilson was urging A.A. members to work harmoniously and positively with the medical and psychiatric professionals like Dr. Silkworth, Sister Ignatia, and Dr. Tiebout (early friends of A.A.) in whatever ways were possible. While it was and remains good advice for A.A. members, it is also a message well-given today to the many professionals who are working with alcoholics, their families, friends, and employers.

There is today (as there always has been) much to learn from A.A. members' hope, strength, and experience. Especially when it comes to the topic of relapse.

With as much information on alcoholism being presented today as there is, it is important that anyone who would help not be partial to a single view to the neglect of truth and help from other quarters. There is enough research and personal experience in A.A. — as there is in psychiatry and other fields of medicine — available today indicating some definite factors that aid the alcoholic in avoiding relapse. They should not be overlooked.

Dr. Weisman and Ms. Robe have used different tones in presenting their material, but in so doing, they have written a lucid, rounded, and highly informative work on an important subject in the field of alcoholism.

THE JOHNSON INSTITUTE

relapse

MAXWELL N. WEISMAN, M.D.

INTRODUCTION

While it may clearly be argued that all human beings are, in the final analysis, responsible for their lives and actions,[1] people who are victims of disease are generally considered in a different light. Certainly the child with sickle-cell anemia or the adult who begins to show signs of Huntington's chorea is absolved of responsibility for the condition. Obviously the element of choice is lacking in such inherited diseases. It is lacking in other diseases as well. Disease is never really "chosen."

Someone seems to be leading an average, healthful, possibly even exemplary existence when a change occurs in one's body and behavior, a change which may then be diagnosed as leukemia, for example, or pneumonia. In many diseases the etiology is unknown as in multiple sclerosis and arthritis. In other illnesses, if we use the public health model, the agent pathogen may be known — *i.e.,* alcohol in alcoholism and mycobacterium in tuberculosis — but the presence of the pathogen, while necessary, is not alone sufficient to produce the signs and symptoms of the disease. Most adults drink alcohol or, in urban communities, have the tubercle bacillus within them but do not succumb to the disease.

Some diseases are acute, like pneumonia, for which cures are known while other illnesses are chronic and progressive, like diabetes and alcoholism, for which no cure is known. Some diseases like measles occur only once in any individual. Others show a high rate of relapse. Coronary infarction and alcoholism are in the latter category.

DEFINITIONS OF ALCOHOLISM

In spite of the voluminous literature on alcoholism, relatively little has been written on the subject of relapse. There is also no universally agreed upon definition of the term as it applies to alcoholism.

Medical dictionaries define relapse generally as "the return of the symptoms of a disease after convalescence has begun"[2] or similarly, "the return of symptoms and signs of a disease after apparent recovery."[3]

With regard to alcoholism, the American Medical Association (AMA) states "It should be approached in much the same manner as are other chronic and relapsing medical conditions. The aim of treatment is then viewed more as one of control than cure. Abstinence is sought as a primary objective...."[4] The American Medical Society on Alcoholism (AMSA) goes further and states, "Because relapse is possible even after many years of remission, we cannot use the term 'cure'.... One index for recovery is sobriety; comfortable abstinence from alcohol and/or other dependency-producing drugs."[5]

Since the concept of "convalescence" or "apparent recovery" in the above definitions of relapse thus necessarily involves abstinence, a single drink would represent a "return of the signs of the disease." The accumulated wisdom of Alcoholics Anonymous (A.A.), distilled from thousands of case histories, states it very simply: "For an alcoholic one drink is too many and a thousand are not enough."[6] A.A. literature refers to relapse as "slips," as "falling back into the old drinking patterns."[7]

Unfortunately, these A.A. statements may be misunderstood and misinterpreted. Alcoholics themselves may even attempt to refute them in the interest of self-confusion and denial of their illness. An example: after a brief or longer period of abstinence many alcoholics will "suddenly" decide to test the above dictum and take a drink. Can this experience of a single drink (or more) be called a "relapse" when, as often happens, alcoholics may not immediately suffer any observed harmful consequences, *i.e.,* neither intoxication nor any other obvious "signs and symptoms of the disease?"

In some individuals this "controlled" drinking period may last for a considerable period of time, weeks or months, even extending into a year or more. Some investigators have therefore concluded that a return to drinking *may* be an acceptable and safe alternative to abstinence for some alcoholics.[8] The latest study, however, a ten-year follow-up reevaluation of an experiment which seemed to support such a conclusion effectively refutes it. "Of the original 20 experimental subjects... only one, who apparently had not experienced physical withdrawal symptoms maintained a pattern of controlled drinking." Six decided to become abstinent and all 13 others relapsed in that there was a "return of symptoms and signs of the disease." (Nine went on to excessive drinking in spite of repeated damaging consequences and four died from alcohol-related causes.)[9]

It is, then, important to recognize the validity of A.A. experience, that when an alcoholic takes one drink, the process of relapse has already begun. Where a pattern of controlled drinking may be maintained as in the single subject above, the diagnosis of alcoholism may be questionable. Alternatively, since rare spontaneous recoveries without treatment have been known to occur in other diseases, including cancer, one may theorize that a similar phenomenon may occur with alcoholics. However, in the light of the impossibility of making a prediction and anticipating such a result with any degree of accuracy, for any physician or other professional therapist to ignore the need for treatment, once the diagnosis of alcoholism is made, would be tantamount to malpractice.

The term *relapse* may, strictly speaking, not be applicable to many alcoholics in the early stage of their A.A. attendance. They cease drinking and thus seem to be "convalescing" or in "apparent recovery." They attend several meetings over several days; but then, they return to drinking. What happened? The most obvious explanation seems to be that they were attending A.A. meetings while *still* drinking. They came to A.A. hoping to find a way to continue drinking in a "controlled" fashion without suffering harmful or painful consequences. Not finding it, they experimented with a brief "respite" from drinking for a few days or even weeks to address perhaps the need to feel better physically, to "get things back together," to pay a few bills, and even to convince themselves and others they were not really alcoholics. Since their need to stop drinking — and especially how to do it — had not been addressed, the experiment soon ended. Such a return to drinking is not technically a relapse, since a commitment to abstinence had never really been made and no change toward recovery had begun. Such individuals are actually continuous, or, more literally, continual drinkers with interruptions (or what have been called "sabbaticals") in their drinking.

Accurate figures about percentages of relapse are, at best, difficult to calculate. In addition, there are very few prospective studies covering any appreciable period of time. Those by George Vaillant[10] and his colleagues are among the very best. Alcoholics, of course, unfortunately disappear not only from records but also from sight. They are frequently lost in "geographic cures" with no way for a researcher to know whether this disappearance was followed by relapse, recovery, or premature eternal rest. Besides, researchers rarely establish objective evidence of relapse by taking blood alcohol levels. They usually rely on self-reporting, but alcoholics are notorious for *under*reporting how much they drink. Fortunately the existence of alcohol-related problems, relatively easily ascertainable, are by definition correlated with drinking.

The time length of abstinence clearly affects the percentage of relapse. The best studies indicate that the longer an alcoholic remains sober, the less the risk of relapse. The classic survey of nearly 25,000 members in A.A. revealed that relapse occurred in almost 60 percent of those who had been sober for only one year but fell to less than 10 percent among those who had maintained sobriety for five years or more.[11]

DENIAL: CUNNING, BAFFLING, POWERFUL

Denial is a fascinating phenomenon. Many people who are close to an alcoholic have come to realize that the drinking alcoholic is a sick individual. Many therapists and researchers have accepted the disease concept of alcoholism, a dependence on alcohol that involves an aberrant psychological drive or a cellular, biochemical maladaptation, or both so that the drug is required for the individual to function "normally." Many family members and friends of alcoholics who are not alcoholics themselves have moved beyond asking the fruitless and, at present, unanswerable question "Why can't he or she control his or her drinking the way I can?" to a sad recognition of the compulsive nature of the illness. But what is often astonishing and utterly incomprehensible to all these people is that alcoholics can *deny* having a problem of control in spite of repeated evidence to the contrary.

How often has one heard an alcoholic resist treatment and say, "I can take it or leave it, I have no problem with alcohol," and this, even in the midst of intoxication and a horrendous crisis. Surely, one feels, the alcoholic must be *aware* of the reality. It is, then, small wonder that close family members and dedicated, compassionate physicians and counselors feel frustrated and angry. Indeed, some ultimately reject the alcoholic as "uncooperative," "unmotivated," and "hopeless."

The conviction has even developed that there must be a pre-existing alcoholic personality characterized by insatiable dependency needs, selfishness, irresponsibility, moodiness or extreme emotional lability, poor judgment, inability to form good personal relations, self-destructiveness, and perfectionism. Nothing could be further from the truth. While these traits are, indeed, found in many alcoholics, they are largely the *results* of alcoholism and are often the direct consequence of an alcoholic existence added or grafted on to pre-existing traits.

When someone denies an allegation about oneself which is clearly a fact and of which he or she is aware, that person is defined as lying. In the case of alcoholism the process is not that simple. Careful, empathic history-taking will often reveal that the alcoholic, on *some* level of consciousness is aware that the difficulty, the harm, the crisis, stems directly from the excessive use of alcohol. The statement is often made that "the alcoholic is the last to know he or she has lost control." On the contrary, in one sense, the alcoholic may be the first to know and yet also does not know. There is a dialectical unity of opposing forces. The denial, then, stems not from any conscious lying but from the strength of an unconscious defense mechanism which prevents this awareness from surfacing. It remains deeply hidden in the unconscious to prevent the intolerable anxiety which would otherwise ensue. For recovery to take place, this denial must be pierced and the alcoholic must "surrender" to accepting his or her condition.

The process of surrender, however, is just as unconscious as the mechanism of denial.[12] It culminates in what is sometimes called the "moment of truth," when the unconscious forces of stubbornness in the face of reality coupled with an infantile grandiosity are confronted by a crisis which has increased to the degree that the conscious mind cannot overcome it. This conflict of opposing forces is resolved by surrender and a new phenomenon emerges — an awareness of powerlessness over alcohol.

DENIAL: THEORY AND OPERATION

An interesting analogy may be made between denial of alcoholism and the denial of physical illness, a condition called *anosognosia.* The latter, like the former, also relates to a medical diagnosis. Etymologically it is "an unawareness of a diseased condition" and is chiefly found in cases of hemiplegia (paralysis) on the left side in which a lesion of the right thalamus of the brain is present. Here the limbs themselves seem to pass out of the patient's consciousness as though they did not exist and the paralysis is consequently denied. Often the bizarre attitudes and behavior which may result are incomprehensible to the observer, just as difficult to understand as a somewhat different phenomenon: the agonizing pain which occurs in the hand or foot of a "phantom limb" after amputation.

In alcoholism, of course, no such specific organic lesion has been described. Instead, however, there are attempts of theoretical constructs such as the Freudian defense mechanisms mentioned above. Here the ego is regarded as the mechanism for becoming aware of stimuli and for storing the resulting experiences in the memory. The ego copes with moderate stimuli by adapting to them and avoids excessive stimuli by "flight." The ego can, at the same time, learn to bring about expedient changes in the external world to its own advantage by appropriate activity.

When, however, the ego is weak or immature as in infancy or early childhood, and traumatic experiences occur, this juxtaposition results in a state of anxiety. Anxiety, of course also occurs in adulthood when the defense system has matured, in *anticipation* of some trauma; then, it is a signal rather than a result of trauma. In any case, when the anxiety cannot be halted, "repression" occurs and results in "not being able to remember." What is "forgotten" becomes truly unconscious. Repression is particularly pertinent in the inhibition of unacceptable sexual impulses. The degree and intensity of denial are an indication of the strength of the impulses that are being denied.

Similarly, denial is widely and commonly used in normal as well as pathological conditions. Because denial is a relatively weak defense and is subject to the bombardment of reality, it cannot repress an experience, an idea, or an affect into the subconscious effectively. Consequently, denial requires considerable "psychic energy" and is maintained only at considerable cost to the functioning individual. Consistent and excessive use of denial may be a significant precipitating factor in the suicide of many alcoholics.

It is often difficult to understand how denial can operate when relapse occurs among alcoholics who have remained abstinent for many years and who have, apparently, been convinced from their own experience and personal growth, of the benefits of sobriety. Here, too, a careful history-taking confirmed by the testimony of many A.A. members reveals that publicly manifested reservations had existed from the very beginning of "recovery" or had gradually developed. Such reservations may pertain to any aspect of reality, whether it is the validity of the disease concept, its applicability to oneself, the phenomenon of loss of control, or any number of other factors. It becomes apparent, then, that the defense of denial, while it is weak in the sense described above, is extremely strong in its capacity to recur or to persist over long periods without being recognized in the exquisite subtlety of its operation. It must be countered with an equally persistent and long-term attack through a focus on a "recognition of necessity." Only when an alcoholic maintains consistently the cognitive awareness of the *necessity* of abstinence can relapse be avoided. Regular and frequent attendance at A.A. meetings, especially at the very beginning of a program of abstinence ("90 meetings in 90 days" is a familiar A.A. saying), and the simple but helpful A.A. slogan "one day at a time" make this recognition of the necessity to avoid the first drink the very foundation of his or her freedom to live and function.

PSYCHOTHERAPY AND TREATMENT

The relative lack of success of psychoanalysis in the treatment of alcoholism may be seen as stemming from the philosophical conception that the weakness of the ego antedates the alcoholism and is etiologically related to the subsequent development of the illness. Regarded as a symptom of an underlying disorder rather than as a primary disease in itself, *alcoholism remains untreated* even if the drinking may be recognized. The patient may verbalize during therapy an awareness of the destructive nature of the drinking and may even acquire considerable "insight" into psychodynamics. If there is a directive component in the treatment, the suggestion may be made, perhaps even with considerable emphasis, that the patient stop drinking, but unless all the necessary forces are mobilized against the alcoholism, the patient will continue to drink, at best intermittently or in binges. The patient may be in such treatment "interminably," often with a succession of psychiatrists. The alcoholic sinks further into despair, and everyone involved — including the psychiatrist — is convinced the alcoholic is indeed hopeless.

Fortunately, a considerable body of evidence now exists both in the annals of Alcoholics Anonymous as well as in professional publications to indicate that susceptible people who start to drink for any reason may become alcoholic and drink compulsively, not simply because of unresolved psychic conflicts. Whatever traumatic experiences may have occured in the past, the addiction to alcohol and the resultant drinking produce their own traumas, physical, emotional, social, and spiritual. These difficultes may then erroneously be confused with pre-existing conditions or traits and then given etiological significance. Only a period of abstinence, sometimes of considerable duration, will make it possible to distinguish the two.

In most cases it is encouraging to note that abstinence is followed by an amazing alleviation and lightening of the destructive consequences of the disease. Improvement occurs partially because of the disappearance of the toxic effects pharmacologically, but also, in no small degree, because of the dramatic change in life style and the restored ability to cope with the daily problems of existence. In most cases, also, however, an on-going program of supportive after-care is essential, with constant vigilance for the manifestations of "stinking thinking" and tendencies to step back to earlier pathological behavior. In some cases where actual psychopathology has been involved, it is vital for a differential diagnosis to be made and psychotherapy to be instituted, sometimes with possibly life-saving neuroleptic medication. When indicated, such medication must be carefully monitored by a physician skilled in the treatment of alcoholism. But it is, perhaps, even more important to correct the erroneous notion that *all* alcoholics need psychotherapy. There is compelling evidence statistically that alcoholics are no more neurotic or psychotic than a random sample of nonalcoholic people. Psychotherapy is no more indicated for alcoholics as a whole than it is for comparable addicted smokers.

ELEMENTS OF A SUCCESSFUL RECOVERY PROGRAM

Many psychiatrists are convinced that the lowest percentage of relapse is found among those who attend Alcoholics Anonymous, especially over a period of time, even if they are forced or required to attend. Records in driving-while-intoxicated (DWI) programs where the courts or licensing authorities mandate regular A.A. attendance for appreciable periods have shown encouragingly low rates of relapse. Similarly, the Federal Aviation Administration's program for the treatment and rehabilitation of alcoholic commercial airline pilots, which requires A.A. attendance and monitoring for at least two years, is astonishingly successful.

What can treatment personnel learn from A.A. and why is it so successful with a condition formerly regarded as "hopeless"? A.A. was started in 1935, and a voluminous literature has been written around it since then. It is rewarding for therapists to study it in detail, but there is surely no substitute for actual attendance at A.A. meetings to see and hear the program, personally, in action. The following points, however, may be mentioned.

First, the *disease concept* lies at the basis of A.A. understanding of the nature of alcoholism and surely must be the cornerstone of every treatment program which hopes to lower the percentage of relapse. The medical profession, extending back through the Middle Ages to Graeco-

Roman times, had recognized an individual's dependence on alcohol as a disease but social attitudes militated against wide acceptance of that concept. In 1956 the American Medical Association issued a policy statement reminding physicians that alcoholism is indeed a disease, not because it is advantageous to regard it as such, but because it fulfills all the criteria applied to other diseases. Certainly, there are advantages to using the disease concept: viewing alcoholism as an illness may certainly inspire hope of recovery, remove the moral stigma, facilitate help, and stimulate research for more effective treatment. But these are merely fringe benefits, however valuable they are. The disease concept is based on objective, scientific evidence that alcoholism, like all other disease, has a clearly definable set of signs and symptoms[13] (note the definition of relapse above) and a well-defined natural history.[14] It can readily be diagnosed by knowledgeable and competent individuals whose rate of concordance in this disease is higher than for many other diseases. In addition, more fortunately than with many other conditions, an effective treatment *is* known, namely abstinence from alcohol. As in many other chronic diseases (*e.g.,* diabetes and arthritis), no cure is as yet known that will restore the alcoholic to the premorbid condition of being able to drink with impunity.

A second factor that treatment personnel can learn from A.A., undoubtedly, is that in A.A. membership, there is a substitute for the dependence on alcohol. The *Twelve Steps* of A.A. provide for the alcoholic what he or she had sought in alcohol but never really secured. In A.A., there is now a fellowship, a loss of isolation, an increase in self-esteem, the lifting of the burdens of guilt, a meaning and purpose in life, and a source of help for the future. While other involvements, such as churches and civic organizations, may also provide these same elements, A.A. focuses specifically on the needs of alcoholics, and hence, is infinitely more successful. A 30-year prospective study of a community sample of alcoholics has shown that more individuals found help in A.A. than even through specialized, *professional,* clinical treatment.[15]

A third aspect of a successful program of recovery which reduces the risk of relapse is one which constantly emphasizes the pain of drinking while revealing the joy and pleasure of abstinence. Alcoholics, of course, may return to drinking even though they are obviously physically sickened in the process. They may not only get gastritis and vomit, for example, but often develop painful gastrointestinal, bleeding ulcers. Denial in these individuals, however, is so powerful a mechanism and the need or desire for alcohol is so strong, that many will continue to drink even to the point of death. In such cases a program which utilizes conscious, cognitive processes to remind the alcoholic of what may be in store serves as a deterrent to drinking and facilitates the growth of skills to cope with impulses to drink. Sharing and hearing "drunkalogs" at A.A. meetings serve this function as does the oft-heard expression, "Nothing is so bad that a drink won't make it worse." The use of disulfiram (Antabuse), a drug which produces severe physical reactions if alcohol is consumed, also supports the internalization of the desire not to drink. Such "negative" activities alone, however, are far less effective and may even be completely useless and, perhaps, destructive unless they simultaneously incorporate the positive reinforcement of awareness of successes achieved through sobriety. Here, too, A.A. meetings provide such positive experience through the vicarious successes of others. Fortunately, personal sobriety is its own "reinforcer" since almost everything that went wrong because of drinking tends to get better with continued abstinence and treatment.

Finally a comprehensive program for recovery must recognize the role of the alcoholic's surroundings in influencing a return to drinking. Here the family, in the broadest sense of the term, is crucial. It touches the alcoholic in almost every aspect of existence: physical, mental, and spiritual. It is a reverberating system in which every unit particle, every individual, interacts with every other — economically, psychologically, and socially. Small wonder, then, that Al-Anon and Alateen could play so important a role not only for the family members but for the alcoholic, too, in maintaining harmony, well-being, and a stable, healthy, environment. Such a support system, however, must extend throughout the warp and woof of the entire social fabric, penetrating industry, the school system, including professional structures, the criminal justice system, the social welfare system, the health industry complex, the leisure and entertainment world, and in fact, all else. In a sense, every individual coming in close and intimate contact with an alcoholic is touched by the illness and consciously or unconsciously may be changed by the disease process. Thus, the treatment program itself may more markedly reduce the risk of relapse by encouraging change in the alcoholic's surroundings. It must, for example, work with the spouse to refuse to be an "enabler" of continued drinking, and with the employer to retain a recovered alcoholic on the job, but with more clearly spelled-out limits of behavior, in both cases supporting the growth of responsibility in the alcoholic.

PSYCHOLOGICAL PROBLEMS CAN AFFECT RELAPSE

It is all too easy to be critical of psychiatric — and especially psychoanalytic — concepts relating to the nature and treatment of alcoholism. Standard psychiatric interpretation views alcoholism as a symptom of underlying unconscious psychic conflict or trauma, and it generally focuses on the acquisition of psychological insight before the patient can recover. Recovery then, in this view, implies cure when physical health permits the option of a return to social drinking. What is sad is the fact that so many psychiatrists fail to recognize the poor track record they have in attempting to treat alcoholics with such an approach, as they delve into areas like oedipal problems or penis envy, while the patient continues to drink and die of the disease. What may be even sadder is that keenly devastating scorn and ridicule may be heaped on legitimate and helpful psychiatric treatment by a popular speaker on alcoholism. "Wowing an audience" with a title such as "My Mother Had Cold Hands" is not helpful to anyone.

There is no doubt that psychological considerations *are* involved in the etiology of the disease (physical, mental, and spiritual)[16] and certainly in *starting* to drink again in a *relapse.* Jellinek recognized this when he stated the "psychological formulations as to the beginning of alcoholism are much more satisfactory than the pathophysiological ones, but this refers to the initiating mechanisms only."[17]

With such an understanding of relapse, it is clear that the resumption of drinking begins some time *before* the actual "first drink." Even an "impulse" can thus be seen as the product of antecedent mental changes based of course on physiological processes which nevertheless render the alcoholic "powerless" or "helpless" in managing an environment where alcohol is not only available, but acceptable as a mood-changer. Thus, it is logical to ask, "Can one detect a pattern in attitudes and expressed behavior which antedates that relapsing drink?"

Sobriety in an alcoholic must be understood as a dialectical process. Although some alcoholics report that the desire for a drink has left them, many, perhaps most, report that they experience periods of wanting to drink. In some, the urge may be so intense at times that lurid dreams of drinking may occur. Sometimes the sober alcoholic will awaken in a panic fearing that the dream had been reality.

Sobriety for the alcoholic is, then, an equilibrium, a balance between the forces driving one to drink uncontrollably and the new-found strength to counter them, to keep them in check. The struggle is, at first, conscious but then submerges into the unconscious with the potential of reemerging into frightening reality. It may be triggered by a variety of stimuli which energize the negative forces leading to an actual relapse. The essential state preceeding relapse seems to be one of isolation, of anomie. The existential bonds tying the individual to fellow humans, to one's so-called "higher power," to the mysterious joy of living seem lost or dissolved. The individual is adrift and rudderless and cannot mobilize the positive forces which had so recently been embraced in achieving one's abstinence. As a result, the negative forces become ascendent and powerful enough to effect a relapse.

THE DRY DRUNK

While no objective physiological changes have been identified which are invariably found in such an altered state of consciousness leading to relapse ("building up to a drink" or BUD), suggestions exist that indicate a similarity between this altered state of consciousness and withdrawal phenomenon changes in blood chemistry, for example, those found in hypoglycemia. Such changes have been postulated but none have been definitely shown to be implicated. Nevertheless, heightened feelings of anxiety occur with uncomfortable physical accompaniments such as mild tremors and slight sweating. Vague symptoms of depression surface, with sleeping and eating habits disturbed.

Sleep may be fitful and restless with long periods of insomnia alternating with feelings of exhaustion and excessively deep sleep for hours. Appetite diminishes, meals are missed, or "junk food" is craved. The person feels irritable, is easily moved to anger, and is generally more labile emotionally. A feeling of withdrawal, of boredom and listlessness, of inability to go to A.A. meetings may alternate with intense feelings of resentment against family and friends, indeed of explosive outbursts of violence. With the passage of time a deeper depression ensues, nothing seems worthwhile, and feelings of helplessness and hopelessness take over.

Most of these symptoms are reminiscent, of course, of the period when drinking, and a return to alcohol consumption may even be considered. The alcoholic who may be attending A.A. regularly, even several A.A. meetings a week, is completely unprepared for these symptoms and wonders, "How can these things be happening to me sober?" So alien are these phenomena to expectation when "things have been going so well," and so gradual in onset are they that the alcoholic may again deny their existence although the fact of their development is obvious to his or her family and associates. However, a careful, empathic exploration of these facts and a reassurance that the phenomenon is a well-known entity amenable to successful counter-measures will begin to reverse the process and speed recovery. Untreated, unfortunately, the process is likely to proceed to a relapse into active alcoholism.

Members of A.A. have long been aware of the above progression and have termed it a "dry drunk." They have recognized from their experience the possible influence on its origin of both physical and psychological factors. The acronym H.A.L.T. (avoid being Hungry, Angry, Lonely, and Tired) calls attention to the need for good nutrition, emotional equilibrium, relaxation, recreation, and socialization to prevent a relapse.

Although alcoholism, like coronary artery disease and other chronic conditions, *does* tend to relapse, a "dry drunk" is not inevitable and a relapse *can* be prevented. The history of many alcoholics in A.A. attests to the fact that once they have discovered the fellowship and pursue the program honestly and devotedly, even those who were considered "hopeless," relapsing time and again, now almost miraculously begin to lead lives of increasingly improving quality. How is this change effected?

SELF-KNOWLEDGE AND
A SUPPORT SYSTEM

Obviously, a sensitivity to what is happening to oneself is extremely important, but it does not necessarily develop by itself without external help. Regular communication with and feed-back from a close friend or a knowledgeable family physician or counselor can be enormously helpful. The first signs of "backsliding" and of the destructive behavior mentioned above or of "stinking thinking" can be monitored, discussed, and addressed. A good, firm A.A. sponsor is invaluable. An increase in the frequency of attendance at A.A. meetings will counter the tendency to isolate oneself, and more open sharing at such meetings will usually subdue any tendency to resort to tranquilizers or sedatives as substitutes for alcohol. The use of disulfiram, however, may be extremely supportive of increased motivation for abstinence and control over the impulse to drink.

A support system, which had been largely neglected in the past but which is now recognized as most important to prevent relapse, is the immediate family. Involving the spouse and the children as well as the alcoholic in treatment has become an integral part of many hospital or free-standing alcoholism recovery programs. The implication is *not* that interaction with the spouse or the children is the cause of alcoholism nor, indeed, is *the* cause of drinking, in spite of the feeling of guilt with which many family members may be burdened. On the contrary, it is the alcoholism in the family which is the cause of much of the pathology which *every* family member manifests, spouse and children, just as the direct victim of the disease does.

Although a direct, causal connection cannot be made, it is clear that the family acts as a "system" with an interlacing network of relationships and behaviors which often reinforce the illness. When the husband or wife of an alcoholic, however, becomes involved in treatment for his or her own sake either separately or in conjoint family therapy, one notices significant improvement in the drinking history of the spouse who is an alcoholic.

A FINAL WORD
TO HEALTH CARE PROFESSIONALS

Competent psychiatric diagnosis and therapy is not at odds with the experience, hope, and strength of A.A. members. To the contrary, sound psychiatric theory and practice teach the professional that working with alcoholics can be extraordinarily rewarding. The therapy, very simply, must be congruent to the illness. Thus, medical or psychiatric specialists — all health care professionals, in fact — who deprive themselves of both knowledge and experience of A.A. are thereby limited. Expert as they may be in their own professions, they are still able to enrich their skills through the wisdom and practice of A.A.

Another remarkable phenomenon may occur as the psychotherapist, working with an alcoholic patient by him-

or herself, attends A.A. meetings in order to learn how to prevent a relapse or how to cope with one which has just occurred. Aside from the possible discovery of one's own alcoholism, the psychotherapist begins to recognize his or her own role in the alcoholic's support system, even to the extent of having exercised a possible *negative* influence as an "enabler." The therapist may then be self-encouraged to attend meetings of Al-Anon and to work the Twelve Steps of *that* program for him- or herself. Astonishing consequences have been known to occur even rivalling the positive, personality changes induced by long term psychoanalysis. In any event, this author can only urge his colleagues to embark on the gratifying experience of working through the frustrations and "failures" of the relapsing alcoholic patients to experience the rewards of seeing the success of recovery.

NOTES

1. Samuel Butler, *Erewhon,* 1872. See also Abraham Lincoln, "We Hold the Power and Bear the Responsibility," *Second Annual Message to Congress, December 1, 1862.*
2. *Stedman's Medical Dictionary,* 24th ed. (Baltimore: Williams and Wilkins, 1982).
3. *Blakiston's Gould Medical Dictionary,* 4th ed. (New York: McGraw-Hill, 1979).
4. *Manual on Alcoholism,* 3rd ed. (Chicago: American Medical Association, 1973), 6.
5. *Definition of Recovery, Policy Statement* (New York: American Medical Society in Alcoholism, 1982).
6. *This is A.A.* (New York: Alcoholics Anonymous, World Services, Inc., 1953), 8.
7. *A.A. Memo to an Inmate Who May Be an Alcoholic* (New York: Alcoholics Anonymous, World Services, Inc., 1953), 4.
8. David J. Armor, J. Michael Polich, and Harriet B. Stambul, *Alcoholism and Treatment* (New York: John Wiley and Sons, 1978).
9. Mary L. Pendery, Irving M. Maltzman, and L. Jolyon West, "Controlled Drinking by Alcoholics? New Findings and a Reevaluation of a Major Affirmative Study," *Science* 217(1982):169-175.
10. George E. Vaillant, *The Natural History of Alcoholism* (Cambridge, MA: Harvard University Press, 1983).
11. *Survey of Membership of A.A.* (New York: Alcoholics Anonymous, 1980).

12. H.M. Tiebout, "The Ego Factors in Surrender in Alcoholism," *Journal of Studies on Alcohol* 15(1954):610-621.
13. National Council on Alcoholism, "Criteria for the Diagnosis of Alcoholism," *Annals of Internal Medicine* 77(1972):249-258.
14. Vaillant, *Natural History.*
15. George E. Vaillant and Eva S. Milofsky, "The Natural History of Alcoholism," *Archives of General Psychiatry* 39(1982):127-133.
16. *Alcoholics Anonymous* (New York: Alcoholics Anonymous, 1939).
17. E.M. Jellinek, *The Disease Concept of Alcoholism* (Highland Park, N.J.: Hillhouse Press, 1960), 80.

slips, sobriety and the a.a. program

LUCY BARRY ROBE

INTRODUCTION

To A.A. members, a relapse, also known as a "slip," means simply taking a drink. Because avoiding the first drink is essential to an A.A. member's sobriety, the program's wisdom includes many messages about the first drink: "Stay away from one drink, one day at a time;" "It's the first drink that gets you drunk;" "One drink is too many and a thousand are not enough."

When long-time A.A. members talk about relapses or slips, they invariably talk about denial. All alcoholics suffer from denial and come to A.A. verbalizing it; in one way or another, they challenge the idea that they have the disease. Paradoxically, through working the A.A. program, a recovering alcoholic learns much about the denial system, and in time, denial may seem to disappear. However, it remains in the subconscious mind, and it can leap to life at the most surprising and inconvenient times.

Even after a long period of sobriety, an alcoholic's denial system can be powerful, earnestly defended, and cleverly camouflaged. Once it begins to operate, it will intensify if not detected, confronted, and discarded.

According to observations by A.A. members over nearly five decades, if a recovering alcoholic wants to stay comfortably sober (in contrast to being dry) he or she must change the attitudes and actions integral to the denial system.

ATTITUDES ARE PART OF THE DENIAL SYSTEM

Looking at "the build-up to a drink" or B.U.D., as A.A. members describe the process, the following attitudes about alcoholism can signal that a recovering alcoholic's denial system is operating again, and relapse could be the result.

Internals Often Observed

Mental reservations about being an alcoholic. Once an alcoholic has crossed the invisible line into the chronic phase of drinking, A.A. members' experience is that there is no going back to "normal" drinking. However, a recovering alcoholic with mental reservations may still harbor some "evidence" that maybe he or she does not *really* have the disease. Thus, maybe it can be safe to drink again.

Illusions that alcoholism can be cured. This illusion was bolstered by a 1970s controlled drinking study. This study was seriously challenged in 1982 by a team of doctors and scientists. Virtually all A.A. members with long-term, comfortable sobriety believe that alcoholism is never "cured" — but is arrested by means of abstinence and important changes in attitudes and behavior.

Belief that alcoholism was caused by problems no longer present. This belief implies that the disease may have abated along with the problems, and that it might be safe to try drinking again.

Disappointment in sobriety. A recovering alcoholic can be in danger of relapse if he or she tumbles abruptly — or with inadvertence to warnings — from the legendary euphoria of newcomers to A.A. The same can happen if problems seem to be worse in sobriety than they were during drinking days. Alcoholics are accustomed to drinking in order to cope, and it is tempting to turn back to alcohol for certain (albeit temporary) relief from pain.

Insistence on permanent sobriety. A.A. members stay away from one drink, one day at a time. Asserting that one will absolutely never drink again can lead a recovering alcoholic to believe that he or she has the willpower to conquer alcoholism. Trusting his or her own willpower can "excuse" an alcoholic from attendance at A.A. In time, the denial system may grow to the point that the alcoholic decides to exercise his or her willpower in "controlled drinking."

Drinking reveries. A major task for recovering alcoholics involves learning that they cannot safely drink *any* alcohol. As A.A. members say, "It's the first drink that gets you drunk." A recovering alcoholic can be headed toward relapse if he or she regularly entertains reveries (thoughts or memories) about drinking.

If, with increasing frequency, good times are recalled without the bad, a recovering alcoholic may underestimate the disease's damage. All too soon, the denial system can resurface, and the rosy memories may lead to a drink. A 1940 *Grapevine* (A.A.'s monthly magazine) article on relapse stressed this point, with the writer suggesting that the recovering alcoholic force the recollections of drinking through to the bitter end, whether it be the following morning and its hangover or several years later with all the mess of alcoholic problems. A.A. members now call this "thinking through a drink."

Wish to be able to drink again. In 1965, when researchers Bailey and Leach asked A.A. members with five years' sobriety whether or not they would drink again if they could, nearly three times as many who had relapsed said "yes" as did those with continuous sobriety. If the sober life seems better than the drinking one, a recovering alcoholic with comfortable sobriety would not trade — even if alcohol intake were somehow to become pharmacologically safe for alcoholics.

Complacency about sobriety. If a recovering alcoholic says "It can't happen to me," particularly with conviction, he or she may be headed for trouble. Most A.A. members have heard "slip stories" involving this attitude. Many of the relapsers later say that drinking was the furthest thing from their minds when they took the first drink.

Externals Often Observed

Imposing sobriety on others. These compulsive attempts take the spotlight off the recovering alcoholic's *own* program — *own* need to change — and shroud problems that could lead to a drink with an inappropriate concern for others.

Ashamed to be known as a nondrinker. Some alcoholics inordinately protect themselves after some length of sobriety, from being known as alcoholics in social or work situations that feature regular drinkers. This subtle form of denial may pressure the recovering alcoholic in a social setting to pick up a drink as a safeguard against criticism from companions.

Listening to contradictions. Seriously discussing with or listening to family, friends, and/or co-workers who tell the recovering alcoholic that he or she is not like alcoholics they have known is dangerous. A premise of A.A. membership is that alcoholism is a self-diagnosed disease. The program's Third Tradition states: "...leave it to each newcomer to decide himself whether he [is] an alcoholic." Believing the contradictions of others can weaken a recovering alcoholic's decision to avoid the first drink. And, unfortunately, such critics frequently turn out to be active alcoholics expressing denial of their own alcoholism.

Preserving old patterns. Continuing to socialize with heavy drinkers, particularly without an adequate counterbalance of new, sober friends and their life style is not helpful. Consistently giving priority to attending functions that provide an opportunity to drink over regular meetings of an A.A. group can result in trouble.

An antagonistic mate. A heavy-drinking or alcoholic spouse or mate who refuses to attend A.A. or Al-Anon meetings or any person who resents the recovering alcoholic's time spent at A.A. may become a problem. Having lost his or her best drinking buddy to A.A., the mate can put tremendous pressure on the recovering alcoholic's denial system. The drinking alcoholic mate may want his or her drinking buddy back — thus (even if unconsciously) this person may *want* the recovering alcoholic to drink again.

Considerable contact with heavy-drinking. This situation parallels the problem mentioned above. Recovering alcoholics who work as bartenders and cocktail waitresses are obvious examples in this category. However, no matter *what* the recovering alcoholic's job — from factory assembly line to corporate president — others' constant drinking and/or pressure to drink by co-workers and friends can be a continual threat to sobriety.

Still the host. Some recovering alcoholics consistently encourage others — family, friends, or fellow workers — to drink. Such recovering alcoholics insist on keeping booze at home, allegedly for family members and/or for entertaining. Besides having a supply of liquor (is that not similar to "protecting the supply"?), the alcohol is prominently displayed, such as on a bar, or heavily stocked, often by the case. And all this is done for moderate-drinking family members and friends. Beyond stocking liquor, these hosts may urge others to drink: this includes ordering drinks for others, bringing drinks to others, and pouring drinks for others — particularly stiff ones.

It is not unlike these recovering alcoholics to attempt to conceal their alcoholism from others. In certain situations, some recovering alcoholics feel comfort in holding a glass of ginger ale. This is traditional camouflage at cocktail parties, for it resembles an alcohol drink, and thus deflects potential pressure from strangers — or acquaintances — to have a drink containing alcohol. Nonetheless, regularly concealing the truth from friends cannot only fuel the denial system, it can also leave the door open for drinking again without criticism from a group of unaware friends.

Speculating about amounts. Rationalizing that a drink with a lower alcohol content would be safe: *e.g.,* beer *vs.* whiskey, wine *vs.* vodka is but a step or two away from drinking. This ploy is frequently used by active alcoholics in their desperate attempts to control their drinking. Any A.A. member knows the outcome: the dainty wine glass gives way to a tumbler, followed by a tall water glass; eventually (that night, next day, the following week or month) the wine itself is replaced by distilled spirits. The alcoholic realizes yet again that he or she has lost control.

Redeciding about drinking. If a recovering alcoholic thinks seriously about attempting social drinking, he or she may be headed for a relapse. This is a very serious sign of closeness to relapse.

ATTITUDES ABOUT A.A.

After the late Charles W. Crewe had counseled almost 500 patients in a program for relapsers at Hazelden, he concluded that between 80 and 90 percent of these repeaters to the Minnesota treatment center shared at least one significant characteristic: deficient A.A. attendance.

According to Crewe, this meant either no attendance, brief attendance, or ending participation in the program prior to relapse. These findings will not surprise A.A. members, whose standard fast message to thirsty friends is "Don't drink and go to meetings."

How many recovering alcoholics stay sober without A.A., or without even *trying* A.A.? No one knows, because most responsible alcoholism experts, including those at the Johnson Institute, believe that the A.A. program offers the best-known way to recover comfortably from the disease of alcoholism. Doctors, nurses, other health professionals, clergymen, families, friends, and co-workers who are involved with A.A. members tend to agree, particularly since many find their own comfort in related programs such as Al-Anon and Alateen.

Of course, some alcoholics come to A.A. meetings for only a brief period of time, and they leave to drink again. Doubters often say such things as "I haven't had an accident, yet"; "I haven't beaten up my kids, yet"; "I haven't passed out in public, yet"; and other similar "yets" as they compare themselves to other A.A. members who have had such experiences. Doubters are told by A.A. members that "the door swings both ways." The idea is that when these men and women drink again, they are apt to begin experiencing the "yets" — those drastic incidents that are likely to happen to alcoholics the longer they drink, and which graphically illustrate the disease's progression. If they are lucky, doubters will have heard and learned enough during their brief attendance at A.A. to bring them back to the program when they undergo a "yet" or two. A.A. tradition says that at the very least, A.A. attendance will have spoiled any fun in an alcoholic's drinking.

Irregular attendance at A.A. is considered risky by members with successful sobriety. Irregular attendance means that A.A. does not have top priority; that other members cannot really get to know the recovering alcoholic well; that the erratic attendee may not be in touch with A.A. at the crucial time when the urge to drink hits.

Limited participation in A.A is another danger zone of potential relapse. This kind of member may show up at meetings with some regularity, but his or her participation in the home group is obviously restrained. Habitual signs of limited participation include:

- arriving late, leaving early;

- sitting alone in the back of the room;

- coming to the meeting hall, but skipping the meeting itself in favor of reading A.A. literature or chatting inconsequentially with an A.A. friend who also wants to avoid the actual meeting;

- dodging making any close A.A. friends;

- having no real commitment to a home group, but instead dropping in to meetings at several different groups so nobody really gets to know him or her;

- making excuses for a consistent refusal to make coffee, clean up, speak, chair meetings, hold office, celebrate anniversaries, or do Twelfth Step work.

RELAPSE AND AN ATTITUDE OF DISSATISFACTION

An A.A. member who is overly critical of the program may be headed back to a drink. Particularly if criticisms are unresolved, this member may become convinced that the program is inappropriate for him or her.

Commonly heard criticisms of A.A. by relapsers include:

A general disparagement of the program. Sweeping complaints indicate lack of tolerance in other areas of life as well.

Boredom with A.A. meetings. The complainer may con him- or herself into believing that he or she does not need meetings. A typical complaint: "I'm sick of hearing nothing but drunkalogs." Old-timers tell these complainers that the "how we were" part of a speaker's story keeps the memory green about the drastic effects of alcoholic drinking, that this memory is important to continued sobriety. The complainer may turn this complaint to advantage and find refreshment by trying meetings at a different group, perhaps in addition to attending the regular group. If attendance at a new group is not just an escape from a serious problem that members of the home group are helping him or her to uncover, it should be of benefit. If the discomfort continues, a sponsor can help the complainer figure out what is *really* wrong; so can the Twelve Steps.

Criticism of meetings. Some A.A. members may complain that a group's meetings are not "as good" as those attended elsewhere, such as in a rehab center or a former home town.

By focussing on negative comparisons, a critical member can become so annoyed with the differences that he or she decides it is a waste of time to attend *any* A.A. meetings.

Although other criticisms may seem petty to an outsider, they are not to the critic. These criticisms can include:

the meeting is too big, or too small; inconvenient meeting nights, times, places; too much smoke, or no smoking allowed; real coffee instead of decaf or tea, or vice-versa; shouting a greeting ("Hello, George!") to a speaker, or not shouting a greeting; custom of using last names, or of not using them; meeting format: existence or lack of Step, Tradition, beginner, open discussion, closed discussion, three-speaker meetings; male only, female only meetings; young people's meetings; growth or feelings groups; concurrent meetings of Al-Anon, Alateen, parents of alcoholics, children of alcoholics.

Sometimes a recovering alcoholic is broadly critical of A.A. members and of their groups. This person might make the following complaints about members of A.A. groups that he or she has tried; all indicate a problem with identifying:

much richer than me; much poorer than me; better educated; less well educated; have better jobs; have routine jobs; not enough professionals; too many professionals; everyone's older; everyone's younger; most are married; *happily* married; *unhappily* married; all are straight; too many are gay; most are single; *swinging* single; not enough action; too stodgy; most are men; most are women; most are Black; most are White; most are Hispanic; I'll be recognized if I go to a meeting in my neighborhood; they're too gregarious; too taciturn; too inquisitive; too aloof; give me too many orders; won't tell me what to do; too many newcomers; not enough newcomers; too much long-term sobriety; too much short-term sobriety; too many slips; they're careless of members' anonymity; they won't exchange names and phone numbers because they're too fearful of their anonymity.

Trivial though some of these complaints may seem, all have been seized as reasons for alcoholics to miss A.A. meetings. All are, therefore, at least indirect and partial reasons for slips.

Newcomers are always urged to try as many A.A. groups as possible. Eventually they will begin to identify, and once a compatible group is found, the generalized complaints will diminish, along with the intensity of the denial system.

COMPROMISES CONCERNING A.A.

Members call A.A. "a simple program for complicated people." In theory, its contents are but suggestions. However, most members with comfortable sobriety find that in order to avoid relapse, the following suggestions should be followed as directions. Members who have slipped realize later that trouble stemmed from one or more of the following areas:

Disbelief that one's life is unmanageable. Working the Twelve Steps of A.A. is vital to recovery from alcoholism, beginning with the First Step: "We admitted we were powerless over alcohol — that our lives had become unmanageable." If a recovering alcoholic does not believe that his or her life became unmanageable through alcohol, there is no incentive to change — or to take the next 11 Steps. Without change, a detoxified alcoholic may begin to feel better, then may rationalize that he or she is not, after all, powerless over alcohol. This faulty belief leads right back to a drink.

Comparing instead of identifying. Some recovering alcoholics persist in favorably comparing their own drinking, and its effects, with the experience of other persons at A.A. meetings. Comparisons include quantity drunk regularly and on sprees ("She drank a quart a day — *I* only drank a pint"); breaking the law ("He went to jail four times — *I've* never even been arrested for speeding"); employment problems ("She was fired five times — *I* only lost one job and that wasn't really for drinking"); marital discord ("His wife left him — *mine* is still at home"); academic difficulties ("She couldn't even get through high school — *I'm* a sophomore in college"); family feuds ("His relatives won't speak to him — *mine* hung in with me"); hospitalizations ("She went through three drying out places — *I've* never been put away for drinking"). Through such comparisons, an alcoholic can become convinced that his or her drinking is not as serious as that of others — and thus that it would be okay for *him* or *her* to drink again.

Compromise in working the A.A. program. Compromise means that some suggestions are not followed. For example, an A.A. member may refuse to work certain Steps. Instead, he or she takes the Steps "cafeteria style" — a compromise.

Compromise is dangerous because the Twelve Steps ingeniously follow one another. Sober members constantly use all the Steps to keep themselves sober, and specific Steps can be useful tools to help thirsty members avoid the first drink. If any Steps are skipped during recovery, a member near relapse may not know how to follow other members' emergency suggestions. Many old-timers ask "slippees" which Step they were working on when they picked up a drink. The answer is usually "none." It is particularly dangerous to avoid Steps Four and Five — the housecleaning Steps.

Not practicing the A.A. program. An A.A. member may refuse to *re*take certain Steps, even when other members believe that his or her sobriety is at stake. Members who believe that taking the Steps is a one-shot deal are also compromising — they do not grasp the importance of continual change as vital to continual sobriety.

An A.A. member may refuse to "be an active member" of the Program: speaking, holding office, making coffee, cleaning up, doing Twelfth Step work, telephoning others regularly are common activity examples. Compromise here is dangerous because, if trouble hits, the alcoholic may be too isolated from the group to ask for help in avoiding that first drink.

TWELFTH STEP WORK

Faulty Twelfth Step work. Helping alcoholics get sober and stay sober in A.A. is vital to the program's very existence. However, certain ways of working the Twelfth Step can be dangerous to the Twelfth Stepper's own sobriety.

"Two Stepping" is a term for A.A. members who jump from the First Step right to the Twelfth, ignoring the Steps in between. The Twelfth Stepper's sobriety may be as shakey as that of the newcomer — and *both* may slip. Newcomers who are eager to do Twelfth Step work are usually encouraged to accompany an old-timer.

Some newcomers are excessively zealous too soon about Twelfth Step work. If their efforts fail, they may become upset enough to drink. A.A. members with longer sobriety know that carrying the message itself is the point: the effort counts, not the result. Having this attitude makes so-called "failures" tolerable.

On the one hand, some A.A. members over-invest themselves in trying to rescue other alcoholics, including sponsoring too many newcomers. Multi-sponsorship can keep the sponsor so busy working on some areas of the program necessary for change and growth in those being sponsored that the sponsor's denial system once again begins to emerge.

On the other hand, some alcoholics refuse to even try Twelfth Step work. Such a refusal goes against one of the basic A.A. messages: "I am responsible.... When anyone, anywhere, reaches out for help, I want the hand of A.A. always to be there. And for that: I am responsible." A.A. members believe that they have to give sobriety away in order to keep it. They call this principle "use it or lose it." If *everyone* refused to do Twelfth Step work, the A.A. Program would eventually die out.

OTHER COMMON PITFALLS

Romance or sexual relations with newcomers. Such emotional involvements are particularly dangerous for newcomers, who are simply too sick and vulnerable to make good judgments. *Any* romance can create problems, and problems can lead an alcoholic back to a drink. Casual sexual relations entered under the pretext of "helping someone's recovery" are usually harmful to the emotions of those who are but newly sober. The dishonesty is always harmful to the phony helper.

Mental reservations about A.A. spirituality. In order to stay sober, A.A. members believe that they need to surrender the will that kept them drinking to some sort of Higher Power. This is the basis of the spiritual part of the program.

Lack of honesty (sometimes unconscious). Active alcoholics are characteristically dishonest during their desperate attempts to continue drinking; this habit must change if they are to stay sober.

Lessening of mental discipline. Steps Ten and Eleven suggest daily inventory-taking, meditation, and prayer. They include asking a Higher Power every day for help to stay sober, and then turning problems over to the care of this Higher Power. Some A.A. members find that slacking off on these disciplines leads back to a drink.

THE DRY DRUNK

A.A. members use the term "stinking thinking" when some — or even more ominously, all — of a recovering alcoholic's old attitudes from the drinking days reappear. If the person talks and behaves somewhat as if he or she were still drinking, members call it a "dry drunk." A recovering alcoholic on a dry drunk is, in effect, building up to a drink. He or she *will* drink if a dry drunk runs full course.

How do A.A. members cope with dry drunks to avoid slipping? H.A.L.T. The acronym "H.A.L.T." is a standard emergency tactic. H.A.L.T. means: Am I (or are you) Hungry? Angry? Lonely? Tired?

Hungry. Hungry active alcoholics find quick relief from a drink. Recovering alcoholics may not realize at first — or they may forget — that the urge to drink may simply indicate hunger.

As soon as it is comfortable for the recovering alcoholic, eating habits should be investigated. Are meals regular? Well balanced? Nutritious?

Has the alcoholic on a dry drunk eaten enough that day?

Angry. A.A. members believe that they cannot afford unbridled anger or resentment. Attending an A.A. meeting, discussion with another member or running the problem through the Steps usually relieves the anger enough to ward off drinking. The Serenity Prayer is often the most effective tactic in emergencies.

Lonely. Alcoholics — even bar hoppers — are inherently lonely people. The A.A. Fellowship is designed to alleviate loneliness through meetings, meetings, and more meetings. Using the telephone to call another A.A. member is the best known emergency measure when a recovering alcoholic is about to pick up a drink.

Tired. When they are tired, active alcoholics use booze as a quick "pick-me-up" — traditionally in the evening, frequently at lunch, sometimes in the morning. A recovering alcoholic who craves a drink may simply be tired, and a short nap can alleviate this. However, there is no substitute for adequate sleep patterns.

HOW MANY A.A. MEMBERS SLIP?

The odds for staying sober rise the longer a recovering alcoholic is abstinent in A.A., according to the *1980 Survey of the Membership of A.A.*

Querying 25,000 members revealed that those sober more than five years stand a 92 percent chance of remaining sober in A.A. another year. Odds dip to 86 percent for members sober one to five years, and plunge to 41 percent for those sober less than a year.

Half the newcomers are in A.A., sober or not, for more than three months. Half of these stay sober through the next year.

At a typical A.A. meeting, according to the *Survey,* from 35 to 40 percent of members have been sober less than a year; about the same from one to five years; from 20 to 30 percent have been sober five years or more.

Although A.A members would ideally like to see a 100 percent recovery rate, the current figures are actually quite high. For hundreds of years, the medical profession had no idea how to treat the disease of alcoholism with *any* success. Until A.A., alcoholics who quit drinking solo might have been dry for a while, but most were far from comfortable, happy, or serene.

The miracle is that a way has been found for alcoholics to arrest their disease and still enjoy life — a way that works for any alcoholic who is willing to follow the A.A. Program.

BOTTOM LINES

Nobody is barred from an A.A. meeting after a slip. A lesson *can* be drawn from a slip, both for the alcoholic who drank, and for those who learn enough to stave off slips of their own.

Since A.A. members function by sharing their "experience, strength, and hope" with one another, "You drank for me" is commonly heard at meetings when a member slips.

While helping the relapser to review why he or she picked up the first drink, members concurrently assess their own attitudes toward whatever triggered the person to drink, and then they describe how they handle such situations without drinking.

A slip strongly indicates that the recovering alcoholic must make one or more important changes. If not, he or she will probably drink yet again.

Next time, the A.A. member might not make it back to the program.

For a full list and description of Johnson Institute publications and films, write or call:

JOHNSON INSTITUTE
510 First Avenue North
Minneapolis, MN 55403-1607

1-800-231-5165

IN MN: 1-800-247-0484